Heart On Her Sleeve

Heart On Her Sleeve
By Grace Patterson
Copyright 2024 by Grace Patterson

Illustrations by Fatima Seehar

Published by
Creative Texts Publishers, LLC

PO Box 50
Barto, PA 19504
www.creativetexts.com
Kindle Version

Heart On Her Sleeve

by
Grace Patterson

with illustrations by
Fatima Seehar

Table of Contents

Heart On Her Sleeve

I write poetry when I am broken
I write poetry when I am overwhelmed with joy

I write poetry when I am in love
I write poetry when I am betrayed
I write poetry when my heart is shattered

I write poetry when I am filled with rage

I write poetry when my chest is bursting from anxiety

I write poetry to express the unspoken

I write poetry when the world is
crashing down on me at 3 am

I write poetry to process the chaos in
my own mind

I am quite horrible at communicating my wants, my
needs, and my thoughts to those I love

So instead, I pick up my pen and let the
words flow onto the page

This is the only way I know how to unravel the tangles
in my own mind

I write to heal all the wounds I have gathered so far
from my time on this earth

I hope my writing helps to heal yours as well

Here's to those who wear their hearts on their sleeve

Art and Pain
One of the same
Who would listen?
Who would relate?
If every ounce of my fate
Was soft and kind
Filled with light intertwined
The art needs to feel
Like maybe I have no chance to heal

How can I love
When I'm afraid to fall
To give someone my all
Seems like my inevitable
Downfall

To create
To risk
To give a peak into your crazy mind
In hopes
That the reader finds
Just a brief moment of relief
That they aren't the only one
To hurt so bad they bleed
To die inside and wonder
Why the hell am I still alive?
Suddenly, they feel less alone
When walking through
Emotions they have never known

I loved him for his mind
Intricate and complex
I never knew what I would find next
An endless ocean
Poisoning me like
A deadly potion

He's kind
In a very different way than "nice guys"
There's truth in his eyes
I know I am looking into his soul
He does what he says
A man of his word
He'd go to each end of the world
Just to make sure I felt heard

I recognize something familiar in him
Pain
Barely detectable behind his big smile
I'm certain others wouldn't notice for miles
But I too,
Wear a similar shoe
I wear chains behind my shiny surface
But, keeping our walls up with each other
Would be a huge disservice

Darling, you make them uncomfortable
Your light is something
They want to squash and burry
In the depths of the night
For they fear
If you gain sight
Only you will be left
Dancing under the moonlight

You scare them
The way you wear your clothes
The way you speak your thoughts
Always connecting every dot
To love you
They would have to look within
And go to places they
Have never been

They can't love you
For you hold a mirror
You unintentionally
Make them see clearer
Their failures and dreams
All bursting at the seams
Every time you win
It cuts deep in their skin

Stuck in a dream
Where no one can hear my scream
Hello?
Help?
All I see are faces I do not know
I'm lost
I would pay any cost
To wake up
To be heard
Yet, now my vision is blurred
My words forever slurred
This bad dream
Bursting at every seam

How should I act?
I'm a doll
How should I smile?
I'm a doll
The world makes me feel
So, so small
I hate how they make me play
All I want to do is say
I hate you!
I hate you!
I wish you would all go away
And let me have
All of my desires
From yesterday

And what if I'm scared?
That all my efforts were for nothing
I'm constantly rushing
One project to the next
It's my reflex
I want to succeed
I'll die if I don't
Why am I this way?
I wish I could just say
"I'll see what's next"
I hate that I make life so complex

Stay small
Stay silent
Speak low
Otherwise they will grow
Envious and jealous
It's better to stay small
Keeping up your wall
Is protection for all

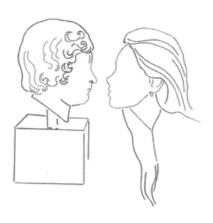

I'm human
I mess up
Say the wrong thing
Laugh at the wrong moment
But then,
They turn me into their opponent
Can't they see I'm human?
Or was I always an object
Expected to be perfect
My flaws forcing them to
Hold their applause

Everything hurts
The way they judge
The way they laugh
It cuts me in half
Can't they see?
All I want is for them to accept
The authentic version of me

Betrayal by a friend
Starting to become a trend
Again and again
My bleeding heart torn apart

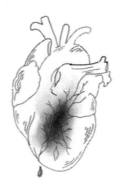

What I love
Creating
Relating to what we all feel
In different capacities
Anger
Envy
Love
While most shove it down
I wear mine
As my crown

The artist
The one that harnesses their emotions
Yet, lets them run free
Like the air and oceans
Creating moments of magic
Finding the beauty
In the tragic

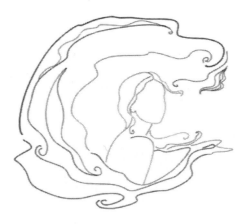

Healing
More than a feeling
A hole spread widely across my soul
Now my only goal
To lose control
To feel free
To allow myself to crash
Over and over
Like the sea

When it's over
Will you forget
Every memory
Time spent
The moments we felt
Totally content
The smiles
The laughs
Perhaps we were always
Meant to collapse

You and me
Can never be "we"
Fire and Ice
Unable to fill our vice
We burn
We freeze
Our love as delicate
As a summer breeze

To create is brave
Shining light onto what others won't say
The artist lays all secrets
Out on a silver tray
Ready to be judged
Ready to be hated
Hoping that what they created
Will find its place
Forcing the reader to come
Face to face with the parts of
Themselves they burry into
Their pillowcase
To create is to show
The ugly
The flaws
The parts of ourselves that deserve no applause

That is art

The truths that come only
From deep within the heart

Shine your light
So others can see
Your spirit
Your fight
The flame within you
That makes you bright
All the things this world
Needs when its dead at night

Things that bring me joy
Twisted into a bitter ploy
Why?
Does other's happiness trigger envy?
A truth denied but known deep inside
Just because we share blood
I won't sit and be judged
An older woman once admired
Now turned into a witch
Someone I fear, no matter how few times
I see her each year

An artist
"A coward"
Someone the world is dying to devour
They cannot stand what lies beneath
Stories
Films
Poems
Art
They will burry you alive
You make them feel like
They are dead inside

"I love you"
Why lie?
Everyday I die inside
Your words kind and soft
Your actions harsh and cold
You had me sold
You were someone I could trust
Now your face fills
Me with deep disgust
"I hate you"
Just say it
Your actions already display it

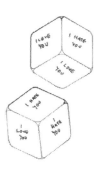

They smile to her face
Even a watchful eye
Would not be able to spot a trace
Of the words they speak
Behind her back
If only for a second, for her sake,
Their act would crack
She's beautiful
Long brunette hair
And totally unaware
Her friends are monsters
Animals hunting their prey
If only, she knew to stay away

On the water
I find my peace
All of my feelings
I need to release
Leave my body
My mind no longer foggy
The water and me
Never disagree

The water
The wind
The sun
The sea
All working together
To set my soul free

They wanted to confine me
I let their words define me
Stupid
Blonde
I never would respond
Their words like swords
Leaving marks as they hit
I let them
Just to avoid conflict
Was it worth it?
Should I yell?
Should I scream?
All you are is petty and mean
Oh, how I wish I was brave enough
To intervene

To create
To risk
To give a peak into your crazy mind
In hopes
That the reader may find
Just a brief
Moment of relief
That they aren't
The only one to hurt so bad
They bleed
To cry so hard
They had to put up a high guard
They suddenly feel less alone
To walk through new emotions
They have never known

Why do I prefer to be alone?
I would much rather remain unknown
Someone that lets them guess
It's safer if people know less
From what I've learned
People are dangerous
They will dress like sheep
Then cut you with a knife
While you sleep

Inspired by the world
Hated by the world
Loved by the world
All at once
Forcing the artist to confront
The art that lies within
Feelings that go
Far deeper than skin

In our dreams
We roam unbound
Exploring realms where truths are found
In dreams, we glimpse what could be
The possibilities that set us free
We fly
Wonder
Explore
Cherishing all that dreams have in store
Leaving us more optimistic than before
Our minds and hearts
Connecting the parts of our desires
That we burry deep
Secrets we cannot keep
While we are asleep

Smile lines
Signs of a good life
So divine
Each crease tells tales of joy and glee
A life well-lived
For all to see
Let them be prominent
Those signs of bliss
A testament to a life that's rich
Embrace each line
For they hold the key
To happiness and a life
That's free

When did life become such a race?
Who can get from place to place
Faster
Better
Always with a smiling face
I want to take up space
In each moment
A slight
Postponement

A Wish
A want
A feeling
A love
A passion
An obsession
One might say
It's all I can think about
Everyday
It's not far away
I keep going
Despite people's dismay
All of my dreams
Are only days away

A lover
A friend
No more wounds to mend
Accepted and cherished
Finally a love
That will not perish

I kept you safe
I protected you
I was elected as the oldest
To be the boldest
You both stand behind
Pretending to be blind
As I shield you like a fortress
Always taking your side
I was never going to allow
A day to come where you cried
Now I wonder why?
I ever even blinked an eye
When the roles reverse
You treat me like a curse

I can be anything you want
Putting your smile above my own
It's not your fault
I became the clown
To protect and manage
The emotions of others
My brother
My mother
Providing temporary relief
To family suffering
It worked
They laughed
They smiled
I did it!
Mission accomplished
I will drown out my own tears
In the shower
Until my voice loses all of its power

I had no choice

I was the oldest
Meant to protect
The role became mine
The clown
Cheering others up while they are down
Everyone likes me this way
I can always make their day
But I'm not the clown
That was never me
Just a way to protect my family

Sometimes I wish
You would remove your mask
So I could see all the secrets that hide
Or
Would they be so dark
You'd be worried
I'd die?
I think it's something we'd both regret
If we didn't try

Broken
As easily as glass
She is shattered in pieces
No repair
Would ever make her feel
That she was rare
For when hands you trust break you
There is nothing on earth
That can ever remake you

Who can she trust?
Just yesterday
It was many
While today is it none
All she hopes for
Is someone she can believe in
That holds truth behind their grin

Love is not simple
She says
It's darkness
Meets light
A hard fight
To see who can
Last in the midst
Of the night

Ultimate highs
Ultimate lows
All places
I have wanted to go
The need to feel it all
Very well may be
My downfall

You and the devil
Are on the same level
Evil and cruel
But trust me, I am no fool
I see your sickness
Your slickness
I see you at war
With all the demons
The reside at your core

Alone
That's how I prefer it
People drain me
And then I am left
It's like they committed theft
Leaving me dry
I wish I knew better
When to say goodbye

Our darkness that we share
Becomes less on our soul to bare
Is it not the goal of life
To take our masks off?
To expose what's underneath
So those close
Can understand us the most

She could never be
What they wanted
The perfect mold
Would eventually unfold
Afterall she was human
She had many flaws
And so they used their jaws
To destroy her
Leaving her for dead
They laughed as she bled

Heart on her sleeve
She always wants to believe
The best
Although, her worried mind
Gives her no rest
To love fully
In a world
So disturbed
Is complicated at best

Monster
That would be too kind
Although, one would
Have to be blind to disagree
Your goal
To tear me down
To suck the air I breathe
Oh monster,
You sorry soul
No matter what you do to me
You will never feel whole

A girl unheard
Her reality blurred
Desires rejected
How could she not be affected?

I can't breathe
They laugh
I plead with them to back down
Within seconds I may drown
They shove me further under
Any love they had for me
Runs free beneath the waters

Anger
Rage
I've been shoving it down deep
Into a mindless cave
It's exploding
I hate you
Yet you attached to me like glue
How do I escape?
You leave me nothing
But weak bones that break

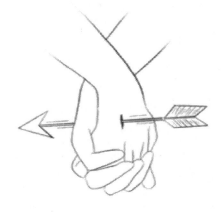

What do they want?
A doormat
Something nice to look at
A smile
Perfect style
I'm tired
I cannot meet the standards required
Messy
Loud
Carefree
I am more like the black sea

She just wanted to follow her dreams
Without others trying to crush them
She was exhausted
Gasping for air
While they sat and glared
They wanted to leave her impaired
So that any dream she dared
Would be washed away
Forever kept at bay

They loved her
Then they hated her
She changed
And they became enraged
She tried to go back
To become what they wanted
But it was too late
They had already decided her fate

Women she admired
Now despised her
They hated what she did
What she said
They did not care
She was half their age
Her presence now filled them with rage
She reminded them of the air
They never breathed and the life
They never lived

Shine your light
So others can see
Your spirit
Your fight
The flame within you
That makes you bright
All the things this world needs
When it's dead at night

Pathetic
All you care about is aesthetic
You're superficial and vain
You lack depth and brain
At the end of the day
None of it
Will ever take away your pain

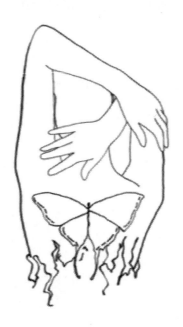

When would she learn
To let things burn
Not everything was meant to last
Some love is meant to be left in the past
To die
Quickly and fast
Leaving nothing but
Memories and ash

Most people she loved
Tended to shove her into a box
Then chain it in locks
They were more comfortable with her there
And they made it
Her burden to bare

Family members
She admired as a child
Suddenly decided she was
Too wild
They hated what she did
What she wore
What she said
Now her love turned to dread
She hated the image of her that they spread
She wanted nothing more
Than to go back to how things were before
But it was too late
The version of her they hated had been sealed
And now was her fate

When love is right
It shines bright
In the dead of night
A midnight kiss
Sweet summer bliss
I just wish it could
Always be like this

The sweet bliss
of this town
I will miss
The way nature sings
The way I watch the birds
Spread their wings
The vast lake
Taking my breath away
I wish I could stay
In this day forever
Tomorrow would be never

Reading
Words on a page
The characters forever
Trapped at that age
Their stories bring me life
They bring me joy
They bring me hope
Because of the writer
My day shines brighter
I want to dance
I want to run
Reading makes me feel
Like my book
Has just begun

How can I experience
Such magic
And extreme tragic
In just one life
Things that break my heart
And things that mend it
I can't comprehend it
How can such joy
And Pain
Exist in one brain

You're the warm summer breeze
You're the sentence I say with ease
You're everything to me
The sun
The moon
The late nights in June
You're the song I sing
Out of tune
You unknowingly heal my every wound
You are the best friend
I never knew

Tears run down my cheeks
As he slowly cups my face
My heart begins to race
Faster
And faster
I have never been in this place
The hands of a loving man
Delicate and kind
I am a flower to him
Fragile
Being gentle with me
Is not something he calls a "hassle"
He wipes my tears
His goal to fix my pain
His presence continues
To rewire my brain

Hello
We started off as strangers
Unaware of the dangers
Of getting too close
A little of you was sweet
A lot of you was poison
A dangerous potion
Stirring all of my emotions
Tainting my soul, my thoughts, my mind
We should have stayed distant
And left "hello" behind

What does it mean to be brave?
Does it mean I must fight back
While they throw me in a grave?
I was taught to play nice
But they take that as a green light
An invite
To throw stones
In hopes they shatter my bones
I want to be brave
I'm not.
I was taught to be nice
No matter what they say
The only thing to do
Is make sure my own daughter
Would never act this way
She will hit back
She will not be someone
That lets others attack

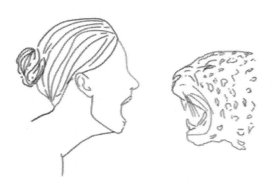

His words
Like honey
Sweet and sticky
Draw me in
Wrapped in their tempting embrace

We should have
Said goodbye sooner
All this has become
Is misery
All that was glittery
Is dead
We should have gotten ahead
While we had a chance
This was our final dance

I want to be there
But when I am
Do they even care?
I don't fit in with a crowd
I try my best
Everything feels like a test
Did I perform?
Did they laugh?
I hope they accept me
Every rejection feels like the death of me

Too weird
I wish I could disappear
Everything I do is wrong
The way I laugh
The way I speak
I pray God would have
Made me more meek
The way I am
Brings me nothing
But critique

A candle's warm embrace
While I find joy in the pages
Words written throughout the ages
A good book can always take you places
Long walks
Nature's beauty all around
Grounding my soul
Reminding me to let go of all control
My heart is at ease
No chaos, just a moment of peace
Candlelight and nature's grasp
Bringing joy and serenity
In this loud and crazy place
Whether it be my legs or my mind
Leading the way to a silent escape
A place to reshape
My mind, my soul
To feel truly whole

Broken
By words
By actions
By strangers
By blood
All of which
Cause me to pour out
In the chaos
Of my own flood

Love
With the right person
Fits like a glove
It's calming
The silence in the midst of a storm
It's warm in the middle of winter
The hug after a long day
A steady love
Who never pushes you away
The flowers bought just to make your day
Listening to the words
You spill in a long-winded way
It's the love you know will always stay

Hating on others
A way to discover
How someone feels about themselves
Do they love the skin they're in?
Do they love the places they have been?

My body feels stolen
Before I was even born
Society put a thorn in my side
Claiming my body
Before it was even mine

I write to explore
My own mind
What will I find?
Poems of pain?
Poems of love?
A mixture of all of the above?
I find out as I go
Letting the emotions spill out that I never show

Big sister
Many responsibilities come with that title
I'm expected to protect
I'm expected to be perfect
The example
Never making a wrong move
I must leave zero room to improve
I show up as the best
Perfect grades
The perfect child
All done with ease
Big sister is my expertise

Life
We love
We lose
We laugh
We cry
We experience pain
That makes us want to die
We drown ourselves in alcohol
To feel some sort of high
Some of us are shy
Some of us loud
Others much too proud
Than the loners who can't seem to fit into any
crowd
All of us different
Yet the same
All looking for someone to explain
This thing we call…
…Life

Feeling invincible
Not afraid to be visible
Nothing can hurt you
You're young
You're brave
Your trust easily misplaced
It's a shame all of that is erased
As you age

I'm afraid to grow old
Will my heart turn cold?
As the world tells me
My value
Becomes low
I'll dream of all those years ago
Of my beauty
Of my face
Of who I was
Before the world
Told me my place

Your charm caused much harm
Your smile made me wild
I felt just like a child
Reckless and free
But you could not be
Honest or loyal
I should have seen
Your words were worthless
Never serving any purpose
My dad always told me
A man without his word is nothing
You'll continue running away from yourself
If I were you- I would run too

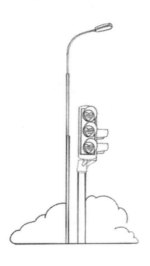

My dream and I
We fight, we argue, we cry
I beg her to leave me
She begs me to believe
Go away! I shout!
But instead she says
Stay and do not doubt
It won't happen I am sure
Though she will not concur
Just look through another door
Your talent has potential to shine
She is sure
Then why won't things align?
It's starting to feel like I'm the punchline
Keep going and have faith
I want to weep and cannot seek you anymore

Well I am here to stay

She is sure, she is confident, and she has no
doubts
That her and I are meant to be
My dream and I

Her heart hardened
And the once bright girl darkened
Probably for the best
She was no longer out west
She had to become tough
So she did- she was no longer a kid
Naive and in bliss
California felt more like a blister
It could burst at any moment if she moved the
wrong way
It was much easier to stay in one lane
And do her best to not become too vain

The sun
The moon
The stars
All working together
To erase my scars

I am
A combination of many things
Laughter and joy
Sorrow and tears
Fear and anxiety
All shoved into one girl
Trying to fit in this society

A shell of my former self
"Be yourself"
But when you are
They hate you
"Be yourself"
Means be who they want
Or else

There is not enough time
For me to do the things I wanna do
To write the books I want to write
Breathe all the air I want to breathe
Be a teacher
Be a poet
Be an actress
Time holds me tightly in its grip
Suffocating my freedom
To explore everything in this life

I'm curled up
On my closet floor
Sickness consumes me
To my core
I can't breathe
Can't think
All I can do
Is cry
Why?
Why?
Would you do this to a girl
Flipping my entire world

Confined by time
Begging for its mercy
Please
Please
One moment more
I am not yet ready
To close this door

Today lovers
Tomorrow enemies
Time slips by
What I would do
To trap it
And make it mine

My life
A horrible construct
Of expectations
Who to be
What to do
I am an animal
Caged at the zoo
Hopefully they will be pleased
With what I do

I am five
Sitting in a hospital waiting room
Wrapped in a beach towel
I can still smell it
Mom cries
It's hard to know what Dad feels
The room is loud
But feels silent
Time frozen
As we wait for news
How can things go from perfect to tragic?
And even now
I am frozen in time
Unable to remember
Anything before the age of five

Daddy can I do it?
I'm a ten-year-old girl that dreams of becoming
an actress
"You can do anything you put your mind to"
I smile.
Maybe he is right
I can be anything I dream
I have my dad on my team

The hours and hours
Put into my craft
Feel like nothing
I love becoming
The best I can be
Preparation makes me free
I can take chances
The scenes become more like dances
The other actor and me
Working together to find harmony

I perform for them
What do they want?
A cheerleader?
A perfect daughter?
Perfect sister?
The real me fading quickly
I really miss her
But these two things cannot co-exist
It's the me they wish
Or the me they dismiss

A big smile
Pom Poms
A large crowd
Parents proud
But at night she cries
Constantly criticized for her size

I'll think of you
When I see a young girl with a broken heart
I'll see myself in her
I'll remember young love
And how it seems it will last forever
I'll remember how you made me laugh
How you made me cry
How you made me wish I could die
How when I called my mom
She actually thought I was dying
But no,
I was just in love with a boy
Who had a problem with lying

As the waves crash the shore
They hope to cause a war
Yet- the land stays still
Unable to be broken
There goes you and me
The land against the sea

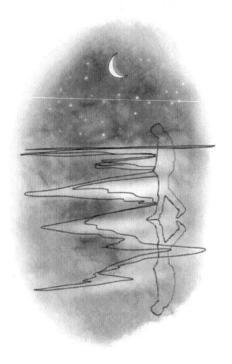

We have a lot in common
With the sea
Unable to see
What lies underneath
Vast and deep
Silent and still while we sleep
All with secrets that we keep

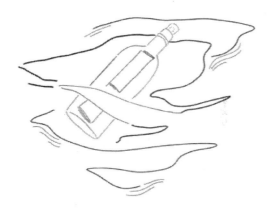

Kiss me slow
Hold me tight
For I've always been afraid
Of what comes in the night

I cling to our love
Too tightly
Fearful it will slip away
What do I have to do
To make you stay?
Will you wake up one day
Deciding it's best
If we go our separate ways

She was fast
Those who loved her
Could never quite catch her
She would be gone in a blur
Leaving them confused
She was as well
Her own emotions scared her
She could never dissect
The things her heart longed for
So instead she decided to protect
Her heart from things that scared her from the
start
Deep feelings
Conversations that went farther than the surface
It wasn't her fault her parents taught her to run
One wrong feeling and they were done

Silenced and ignored

Feelings were stupid and not to be explored
So everything that made her feel
She needed to pretend it wasn't real

Reading
Takes me into a world
Other than mine
I forgot all my worries
My fears
My tears now based in fiction
Instead of reality

Forget this world
This pain
It's all making me go
Insane

Maybe I am insane
I hate it here
Hate it there
I hate it anywhere
The air feels heavy
My soul has been to all these places
Already

She tries to be
A wife
A mother
A sister
A daughter
All the things that they taught her
But when she rests her head at night
Her stomach clinching tight
This is not the life
In which she would find delight

She was sunshine
And darkness
And somehow it charmed us

A bird in a cage
Blue and beautiful
But always in that cage
A prisoner following where
Its captors go
The bird shows no sorrow
Only hoping to make it to tomorrow
I look at the walls around me
No chains
Yet- I might as well be surrounded by flames

I wish I could take your pain
And make it mine
Your life would be fine
While mine would be on the decline
Anything to ensure
Your cure
I never would live one day
Away from you
Please
Please stay
I need you
To be okay

I'm seventeen
Already insecure of how my body curves
I'm in my room taking off my makeup
The mascara runs down my face
Mixtures of blue and brown eyeshadow
Swept away from the day
My boyfriend walks in
Giving me a disapproving stare
Suddenly I'm filled with regret
Removing my mask- a mistake
But it's already too late
"You would keep that on if you loved me"
His words cut deep
It takes everything I am
To not break down and weep
Loving a teenage boy
Just to be treated like his little toy

One day here
The next day there
Tomorrow could be anywhere
My life twists and turns
Filled with things that burn
And just when things settle into silence
I reach for my match
Ready to detach
Leaving flames
My life full of little games

To the givers
To the lovers
To the ones who do too much for others
You carry a heavy weight
You put too much on your plate
To make everyone else's lives great
You are amazing
But remember- it's okay to put yourself first
To clench your own thirst

She has her books
Her words
Her stories
Her mind
All allowing her to find
The pieces of her that were misaligned

I would quit
If I wasn't so obsessed
Give my brain
At least one moment of rest

I over prepare
Why?
I'm terrified of failure
Even the thought of messing up once
Kills me
"Everyone messes up sometimes"
They tell me
But- that thought terrifies me
Every mistake feels like excruciating failure
Every negative thought I've ever had
Is true
I don't deserve anything
Unless I prove
That I can be perfect
I can transform
Into a flawless storm

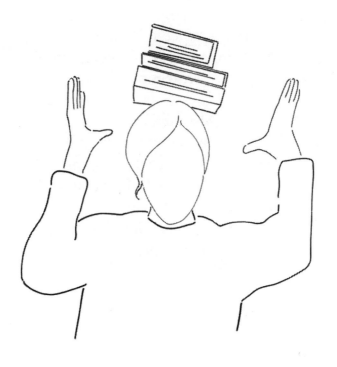

My OCD controls me
1-2-3
Check
1-2-3
Check
1-2-3
Check
The house door is locked
Onto the car
1-2-3
Check
1-2-3
Check
1-2-3
Check
It's locked
I run back one more time to check again
I have to be sure
Every room or car I enter
Must be secure

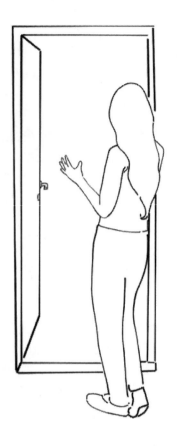

My therapist tells me
To break down
Self-love
Into tiny moments
A warm candle
A fuzzy robe
A delicious meal
Show up for yourself in the little ways
To master the art
Of self-love

I'm in a dim room
I cross my left leg over my right
Then switch
Right over my left
Switch again
Nothing feels comfortable
The woman in the chair across from me stares
I examine her- she has a kind and pretty face
"Pretend I'm him and say what you want to say"
Suddenly my throat closes up
Tears swell into my eyes
Every word I want to say
Stolen from me
I can't speak them
How can words describe the rage

The anger

The pain
How could I ever summarize that I count down
the minutes
until I can cry again?
That I was easily replaced by a man who
claimed to love me?
I have no words for her
But maybe- I have no words for him
Silence
I let it linger
The only thing he ever deserved
Not even a word
Not a breath
Not a second glance
I shed more tears in silence
It answers every question I've ever had

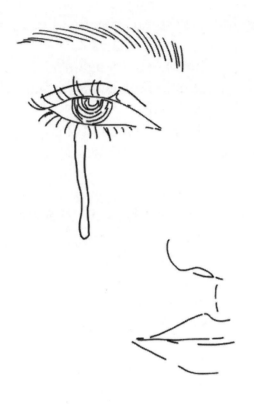

I listen to her
She listens to me
We tell each other what we need
My body

Maybe I'm wrong
Maybe you're right
All of this
Was just a silly fight
Let's just agree to make it end
Before the sun goes down
And it becomes night

I'm sorry
For the things I said
When I was angry
I'm sorry if it made you hate me
Saying things I didn't mean
Caused this mess
To become not so clean
I'm sorry
Nothing can take it back
But I'll do everything I can
To put us back on track

I lie awake
For hours and hours
My mind holds no power
On my ability to sleep
All that is left to do is weep
I am tired
Oh, so tired
My thoughts hold me captive
An eternal jail
I beg
I plead
For my mind to stop being such a mess
I long for just one night of rest
The nights are long
Lonely
I imagine all the sleeping people
I envy them
Their nights are peaceful
While mine are wasteful
Insomnia
I hate you
I wish I could escape you

It's okay to care about the simple things
Peanut butter toast in the morning
Fresh fountain soda at a restaurant
Movie theater popcorn
The little joys
Are the sweet background noise
In this little life

Poetry is for those
Who feel deeply
Never stop wearing your heart on your sleeve

My mind consumed with worry
My vision becoming blurry
I wish I could shut off my brain
Anxiety leaves
An ugly stain

When my hair becomes gray
Will you still want to stay?
When my body is no longer desirable
Will you find my mind to be?
Does your love for me go deeper than what the
world sees?

Is love something
You feel
Something you choose
Or somebody you are deathly afraid to lose?

3 am
I'm awake thinking of something I said
Something I read
That relationship I should have fled
My mind full of "what if's?
What could have been
What should have been
That's why I'm awake
Every decision holds too much stake

What if I could go back?
What would I change?
Would I create more art?
Would I protect my heart?
Or would I let it all fall apart?
Things that are broken
Are a valuable token
When handled with the right care

I felt shattered
Like every piece of me was glass
No one could get near
Sharp edges everywhere
Everyone knows to stay away from glass

It was February
I was overwhelmed by the thought
That love exists
I wrote long lists of all the reasons I loved you
And as quickly as February had started
It ended
Just like our love
A spring of suffering had just begun

Summer came and went
All of my time spent with you
It flew-
I did everything I could to grasp it
For I am not me
Without you

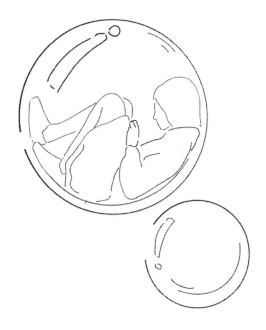

I promised myself
I would never love again
Such a foolish thing
To love
To trust
I crinkled my nose in disgust
My once bleeding heart
Turned to rust

I was naive yet complicated
You were wise
With a rough exterior
Together we were art

I am obsessive and passionate
Pouring myself completely
Into everything I touch

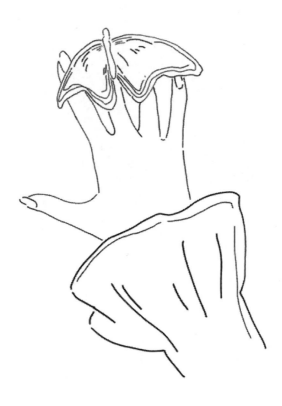

I am nothing when I am not creating
Creation is my air

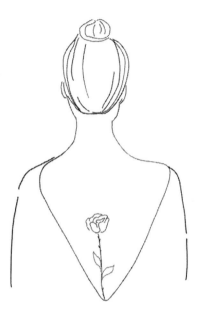

Without a dream
To chase
I am drowning under the weight
Of reality

When I dance
My mind silences
Lost in the rhythm of a song

To dance
To feel something
Not just in your heart
But in your entire body

The worst type of heartbreak
Woman to woman
Friend to friend
Sister to sister
Now nothing but a boiling blister
Unbearable
The bond now never repairable

Sometimes I miss you
A deep longing
But then I remember
The words you spoke
That broke me
Over and over
Your carelessness and pride
The hatred you wear in your eyes
You despise everything I am
I expected it from strangers
But never from you
I keep looking back
in search
of the clues

We will never speak again
I'm at peace with that
It's better than being entertainment
You pick at

There is peace in goodbye
The final wave
The last text
Let what was be just that
Any other words
Fall flat
So let them linger
Now and for eternity

We do not need closure
We need silence
Only when the storm is calm
Can we find the places
We truly belong

Why I love you:
You are gentle
You are strong
You feel and think deeply
You are curious
You are adventurous
You are safe
You are steady
You are all the beautiful things in this life
Wrapped into one being

Poetry
There can be snow in March
Rain in winter
A tsunami in the desert
Land and time are all just words I intertwine

I wish I could do to you
What you did to me
My pain would not be handed out for free
But I am not you
And you are not me
I would never have it in me
To do to you
What you did to me

I am enchanted by life
I am terrified by life
I am excited by life
I am exhausted by life
I am caused pain by life
So many feelings towards this life
The only thing to do
Is live it
Feel it
Let it be everything that it is

I'm wondering
Aimlessly in the dark
Searching for myself

Part of me loved you
Part of me despised you
All of me was hypnotized by you

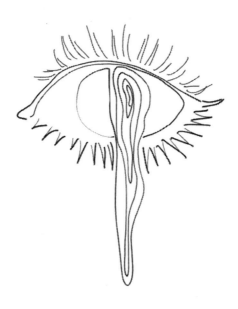

Feeling safe
Something new
I never had a clue
What it meant
To be heard
Every word I spoke as a child
Was exiled
Do my words matter?
Or are they nothing but annoying chatter?

I've lost everything
In the pursuit of my passions
Family
Friends
Romance
I've given it all up
To take a wild chance

I think I've finally learned
I don't have to be like
Everyone else

I remind myself
To be grateful
For the experiences
I've had
Good and bad
Together they add
To my madness

It's okay if they call you weird
You are becoming everything they feared

My hunger to create
Consumes me
Unless I write
I'm left awake
Starving through the night

My childhood
Performing for those with sadness
In their eyes
While masking my own cries

Trading places with my brother
Something I long for
He is the angel I adore
I wish for his life to be easy
Mine to be hard
The oldest sister was always meant
To be her baby brother's guard

I will always do
What no one thinks I can

The most beautiful things in life
Are dreams
Our ability to have them
Our ability to pursue them
Our ability to achieve them
Our ability to pour our hearts and souls
Into a thing we call
A dream

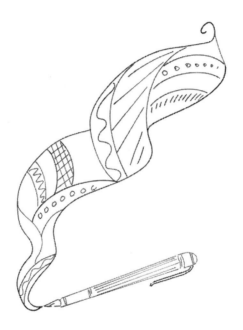

Of course I am scared
I am petrified
Sometimes I am frozen in fear
Everything I desire
Is completely terrifying
But for some reason
I do it anyways

My fear of failure
Guides me through
My darkest days and nights

You cannot live
Your entire life
In fight or flight
At some point you will crash
Losing it all in a flash

You break me
Just to laugh
You are a kid
I am your craft

Let go of the idea
Your life must look a certain way
Stay in places that fill your soul
Run from places that do not
Make you feel whole

Why run
When you could stay?
Life is always better
When you get out of your own way

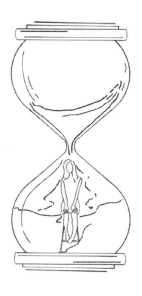

Now nothing but a distant memory
Years ago you were my everything
But- that's the beautiful thing about time
It heals every wound
If you let it
It'll be the thing that keeps you alive
When you feel like you'll barely survive

Why do we choose pain?
It can be hard to explain
But for some of us
Pain is normal
Pain is comfort
Pain is what we have always known
Who are we without it?

The only time I escape myself
Is when I am acting
New clothes
New makeup
New words
Lines given to me in a script
I dive into this new world
This other girl
A moment of escape
Silencing my own thoughts
All at once on Action
Acting is my perfect distraction

This world
How can I love it and hate it?
New life
Death
All of it happening at once
I feel joy
Then pain
Then joy again
I just never know when
This world causes my head to spin

Can you find success with balance in sight
Or must all be risked to reach that height?

Finding myself
In the pages of a script
In the rhymes of a poem
In the words of my favorite book
I am always in search of myself

When I leap
Will I fall
Crashing straight into a wall
The barrier between
Me and my dream
Or when I leap
Will I fly
I'll only ever know if I try

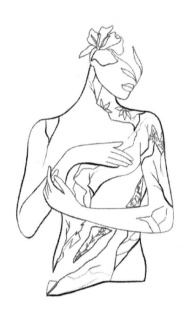

The intense nature of myself
Obsessive
Addictive
Consumed by my desires
To leave fires burning
Behind me on my path

Who I am today
Is not who I was yesterday
Constantly changing
Evolving
Slowly solving the questions I have
About this life
I'm desperate to get it right
If I keep searching
I am sure to gain sight

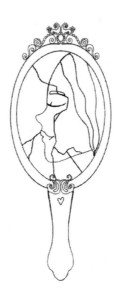

Find someone
Who sees your soul
That will be the greatest love
You have ever known

To begin again
A new life path
A story with no ending yet
You'll never regret
Trying something new
If it leads you back to you

All of my accomplishments
Feel like nothing
I am never satisfied
What else can I do?
I will never view
My goals as complete
I long to pursue new heights
New things
I continue to grow new wings

196

TOGETHER

These words are no longer just mine
They are ours
Here for you when you need them
Here for you when you want them
Here for you when no one else will listen
Together we have shared
This air
We have felt this life and everything it has to offer
Everything it has to take
No one can make it out without a few heartbreaks
Just remember
If it can break
It can mend
This is not the end

ABOUT THE AUTHOR

Grace Patterson is an actress, entrepreneur, film producer and writer. You can catch her in the Hulu film Slotherhouse, Cheer For Your Life, College Professor Obsession, Who Is Killing The Cheerleaders, Pom Pom Murders, Killer Cheerleader, Spring Break Nightmare, Secrets On Greek Row, Loves Fast Lane, Dying For A Bid and more on Lifetime Network. She was a Professional Cheerleader for the Dallas Stars and has over fifteen years of dance experience. Writing has always been one of her main passions since childhood. She is the author of Am I Perfect Yet? Finding Fullness In My Authentic Self and the poetry books: A Woman's World and The Things She Doesn't Say.

ABOUT THE PUBLISHER

Creative Texts is a boutique independent publishing house devoted to high quality content that readers enjoy. We publish best-selling authors such as Jerry D. Young, N.C. Reed, Sean Liscom, Jared McVay, Laurence Dahners, and many more. Our audiobook performers are among the best in the business including Hollywood legends like Barry Corbin and top talent like Christopher Lane, Alyssa Bresnaham, Erin Moon and Graham Hallstead.

Whether its post-apocalyptic or dystopian fiction, biography, history, true crime science fiction, thrillers, or even classic westerns, our goal is to produce highly rated customer preferred content. If there is anything we can do to enhance your reader experience, please contact us directly at info@creativetexts.com. As always, we do appreciate your reviews on your book seller's website.

Finally, if you would like to find more great books like this one, please search for us by name in your favorite search engine or on your bookseller's website to see books by all Creative Texts authors. Thank you for reading.

Made in the USA
Middletown, DE
07 December 2024

66362242R00119